Foods for All Seasons

**Recipes
and photographs
by BÉLA LISCSINSZKY**

Foods for All Seasons

WINTER

in the Golden Dragon Inn

Corvina

Title of the original: Négy évszak ételei
az Aranysárkány vendéglőben · Tél,
Corvina Kiadó, 1986
© Pictures and text: Béla Liscsinszky, 1987
ISBN 963 13 1893 1
ISBN 963 13 1917 2
Translated by Zsuzsa Béres
Design by Zoltán Kemény
CO 2420-h-8789

Foreword

This is a collection of recipes that is primarily intended to provide a visual experience.

I have included a large number of photographs in the book to make it easier for you to select, prepare and serve the dish of your choice. With the help of these pictures even those of you who have done very little cooking will get along splendidly.

The steps in the recipes follow a chronological order, which, of course, does not mean that deviation from this order will necessarily result in failure.

The types of fat listed in the individual recipes (lard, cooking oil, margarine, etc.) cannot be substituted without impairing the fundamental flavour of the dish.

Many recipes call for ground black pepper. Although you may buy ground black pepper at your grocer's, we recommend using a quarter of the indicated amount of freshly ground black pepper instead. It will impart the dish its genuine aroma.

The use of paprika is a more complicated matter. There are many varieties of widely differing quality. Availability and individual preference are also important factors. For these reasons I never specify the quality of paprika in the list of ingredients, I merely indicate whether or not a recipe calls for the sweet or the hot type, or both.

In roasting meat I do not follow the earlier practice of adding water to the oven pan. The meat is roasted in a lightly greased oven pan which considerably reduces cooking time. The result is a tender, juicy roast.

Finally, a few facts about sour cream, a favorite ingredient in Hungarian recipes. Remember
—to always stir a little flour into the sour cream. It will give your sauce a velvety texture.
—prolonged boiling will impair the refreshing tangy taste of sour cream. Add the sour cream only a few minutes before your dish is completed.
The recipes in the book are calculated for four servings.

Béla Liscsinszky

Recipes

Broth à la Petres

Ingredients

1 chicken breast
300 g/10 oz flank of beef
(with bone)
4 quail's eggs
100 g/3½ oz carrots
100 g/3½ oz parsnips
50 g/2 oz celeriac
50 g/2 oz kohlrabi
1 medium onion
2 cloves garlic, salt
3–4 whole black peppers
allspice

To prepare

Clean vegetables, peel onion. Wash beef under running water. Boil water in a small pan, add the quail's eggs and cook for 10 minutes. To facilitate cleaning, place eggs in cold water.

To cook

Place all ingredients, except the quail's eggs, into 2 1/2 qt cold water. Bring to boil, remove froth and cook over low heat for at least 1½ hours. Since the chicken needs less time to cook, remove it as soon as it is tender. Strain soup when beef becomes tender. Bone the meat and dice vegetables and meat to the same size. Replace in soup and add the cooked and peeled quail's eggs. Bring to the boil and season with salt. Serve at once.

Duck liver paté

Ingredients

1 kg/2¼ lb duck's liver
200 g/7 oz smoked bacon
1 tsp paté spice
1 tsp salt
4 eggs
500 ml/1 pint milk

To prepare

Soak liver in milk for a few hours. Slice the smoked bacon very fine or buy sliced bacon. *For the spice mixture* combine and grind a grating of nutmeg, 1 bay leaf, 5 pc allspice, 1 tsp marjoram, 5 pc juniper berries, 1 tsp coriander seed, 1 tsp whole black peppers and 1 tsp thyme.

To cook

Drain liver and put through mincer. Combine with 4 whole eggs, 1 tsp paté seasoning and 1 tsp salt. Put them through a blender and pour mixture into loaf pan lined with bacon slices. Cover with bacon slices. Tightly cover the loaf pan with aluminium foil. Preheat oven to 150°C/300°F, place the pan of paté in a dish half filled with hot water and bake for 1½ hours. Cool and refrigerate. Slice to individual servings of about 2 cm/1 in thick.

1. Lining loaf pan with bacon
2. Filling pan with the liver
3. Covering with bacon
4. Covering with aluminium foil

Lettuce with mustard dressing

Ingredients

2 heads lettuce
2 tbsp mustard
100 ml/½ cup salad oil
100 ml/½ cup dry white wine
ground black pepper, salt
1 egg

12

To prepare

Separate lettuce leaves and wash thoroughly. Combine mustard, salt and black pepper. Add oil drop by drop, stirring constantly. The mustard and oil must form a mixture of uniform consistency. Thin mustard cream with the white wine. Place lettuce on a small plate, sprinkle with mustard dressing and garnish with grated hard-boiled eggs. Serve as a side dish with roast beef and fried meats.

Ingredients

1 breast of goose
800 g/1¾ lb potatoes
5 medium onions
1 bunch parsley, 4 cloves garlic
salt, ground black pepper
marjoram

To prepare

Peel potatoes and onion and cut
into wedges. Season with salt
and pepper.
Rub breast of goose with salt
half an hour before cooking and
sprinkle with marjoram.
Finely chop garlic and parsley.

To cook

Place breast of goose skin down
in larded pan. Roast in medium
hot oven for 45 to 50 minutes.
Turn and add onion and
potatoes. Continue to roast until
both meat and garnishes are
baked.
Baste frequently.
To serve, slice the meat and
carefully combine garnishes
with garlic and parsley mixture.

Breast of goose
with roast potatoes

15

Juniper sirloin steak

Ingredients

600 g/1½ lb sirloin steak
150 g/5 oz gherkins
2 medium onions, 5 capers
1 tsp dried tarragon
1 tbsp tarragon vinegar
1 tsp ground juniper berries
salt, ground black pepper
1 tbsp mustard
100 g/4 oz chicken liver
300 g/10 oz spaghetti
50 g/2 oz butter
200 ml/1 cup cooking oil
2 bay leaves
1 bunch parsley
100 ml/½ cup red wine

To prepare

Cut sirloin steak into 4 slices of equal thickness. Sprinkle with the ground juniper berries, pour just enough cooking oil over it to cover it, and marinate with a few bay leaves in the refrigerator for 2 to 3 days. Cook the chicken liver in a little water until tender, about 10 to 15 minutes. Cool and dice finely. Chop the onion, capers and parsley finely and grate the gherkins. Cook the spaghetti in salted water, drain, rinse combine with a little melted butter and keep warm until serving.

To cook

Sauté the onion in butter until golden brown. Add the gherkins, capers, chicken liver, tarragon, tarragon vinegar and parsley. Season with salt, ground black pepper and ground juniper berries. Pour in the red wine and simmer for 10 minutes. Add mustard and finish cooking. Remove the meat from marinade and drain. Fry both sides quickly or grill. Turn meat only when one side is fully done. Too much turning will impair the tenderness.
Serve the spaghetti as a side dish with the sirloin steak topped with the juniper ragout.

Rabbit paprikash

Ingredients

1 kg/2½ lb rabbit, skinned and drawn
4 medium onions, 1 tbsp lard
1 tbsp sweet paprika
1 tbsp flour
salt, 300 g/10 oz flour
3 eggs, 200 ml/1 cup sour cream

To prepare

Cut the rabbit, unboned, into 60–70 g/2–3 oz pieces.
For the galushka dumplings combine 300 g/10 oz flour with 3 whole eggs, salt and a little water. Skin and dice the onion.

To cook

Sauté the onion in a little lard. Add the pieces of rabbit and brown over high heat, stirring constantly. Sprinkle with paprika and salt, cover and cook in a little water until tender. Finally, bring to the boil with a smooth mixture of 1 tbsp flour and the sour cream. Serve with *galushka* dumplings. Make small dumplings and drop them into boiling salted water in two batches. Drain and toss in a little lard.

Eel with chive sauce

Ingredients

800 g/1¾ lb eel
50 g/2 oz onion, 1 bay leaf
100 ml/½ cup dry white wine
salt, ground black pepper
whole black pepper
1 bunch chives, 2 tbsp flour
50 g/2 oz butter
200 ml/1 cup heavy cream
½ lemon, 300 g/10 oz French
bread

To prepare

Cut cleaned eel into 3–4 cm
(1–2 in) pieces.
Peel and slice onion. Chop the
chives.

To cook

Place eel in buttered dish. Add
whole pepper, onion and bay
leaf. Sprinkle with lemon juice,
add the white wine and enough
water to cover. Cook over low
heat until tender.
Brown flour in 1 tbsp butter.
Add the chopped chives, stir
a few times and add the heavy
cream and eel broth. Boil
thoroughly and season with salt
and ground black pepper.
Serve eel on top of slices of
French bread fried on both sides
in butter. Garnish with the chive
sauce.

Venison, great hunter style

Ingredients

600 g/1¼ lb shoulder of venison
200 g/7 oz mushrooms
300 g/10 oz orange
3 medium onions
50 g/2 oz smoked bacon
1 tbsp cranberry jam
salt, ground black pepper
thyme, 200 ml/1 cup dry red
wine

To prepare

Slice the meat, then cut the
slices into strips. Dice the onion
and the smoked bacon. Slice the
cleaned mushrooms and
orange.

To cook

Fry the bacon and sauté the
onions in fat. Add cranberry
jam, sprinkle with thyme and
pour in wine.
Cook over high heat for a few
minutes and add the meat. Season with salt and pepper and
cook until tender, stirring frequently. (Replace stewing broth
with water as necessary, but
never add more than 100 ml/
½ cup at a time). Finally, stir in
the mushrooms and the orange.
Simmer for another 10 minutes
and serve with potato dough-
nuts.

Potato doughnuts
Ingredients: 500 g/1 lb potatoes,
2 eggs, 50 g/2 oz flour, salt,
ground nutmeg, 300 ml/1½
cups oil for frying
Wash, cook and mash the
potatoes. Season with salt and
ground nutmeg. Knead with the
eggs and flour. Dip a tablespoon
in oil and cut dumplings out of
the dough. Fry until crispy golden brown in hot cooking oil.

Pork liver,
Périgord style

Ingredients

600 g/1¼ lb pork liver
2 tbsp lard
100 g/4 oz smoked
garlic sausage
50 g/2 oz tinned sweet
corn
50 g/2 oz marinated or pickled
green pepper
50 g/2 oz pickled onions
1 bunch parsley, salt
ground black pepper, marjoram
tarragon, 500 g/l lb potatoes

To prepare

Thinly slice the liver,
dice the sausage
and chop the parsley.

To cook

Place sausage
in 1 tbsp hot lard.
Add the sweet corn,
the diced marinated
or pickled green pepper
and finally the pickled
onions, together
with its juice.

Season with black
pepper,
marjoram, tarragon
and parsley.
Cook for 5 to 6 minutes.
Set aside and keep warm
until serving time.
Just before serving,
fry the liver in a little
hot lard in a pan or on
a grill rack.
Salt after cooking
and serve
with the Périgord ragout.

Assorted strudel

Ingredients

3 packets ready-to-use strudel dough (makes 12 strudels)
50 g/2 oz butter
250 g/8 oz cottage cheese
1 lemon
2 tsp vanilla sugar, 1 egg
100 ml/½ cup sour cream
150 g/5 oz ground poppy seed
50 g/2 oz raisins, soaked
500 g/1 lb squash
500 g/1 lb apples
150 g/5 oz ground walnut
1 tsp ground cinnamon
450 g/1 lb granulated sugar
150 g/5 oz castor sugar

To prepare

Cottage cheese filling: Put cottage cheese through a potato masher. Combine sour cream with 1 whole egg, 100 g/4 oz granulated sugar and soaked raisins. Add the cottage cheese, the grated lemon rind and work together with your hands.
Squash-poppyseed filling: Clean pumpkin, scoop out center and grate the pulp. Combine with 200 g/7 oz granulated sugar and let stand for ½ hour. Add ground poppy seed and 100 g/3½ oz castor sugar and work together with your fingers.
Apple filling: Peel and grate the apple. Combine with 150 g/5 oz granulated sugar and let stand for ½ hour. Squeeze out juice and stir in the ground walnut and the ground cinnamon.
Place 2 strudel doughs at a time over a cloth napkin. Sprinkle with melted butter and spread fillings alternately over the surface of the dough. Roll up strudel with the help of the cloth napkin, never actually touching the dough itself. Slide the long cylinders onto a greased baking sheet and bake in a moderate oven for about 15 minutes. Sprinkle with castor sugar.

Fish soup

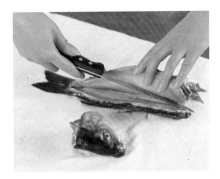

Ingredients

1 [1½ kg/3 lb] carp
5 large onions
40 g/1½ oz sweet paprika
1 tbsp hot paprika
200 g/7 oz tinned letcho* *or:*
200 g/7 oz fresh green peppers
and tomatoes
salt to taste

To prepare:

Spread a sheet of paper on
a firm work surface, so that the
fish will not slip from your hand
while you are cleaning it. Grasp
the carp firmly near the base of
its tail and scrape off the scales.
Rinse in lukewarm water. Do not
wash the fish after it has been
cut up as this impairs the
flavour of the soup. Next cut the
entire length of the belly and remove the entrails. Set aside the
roll, milk and liver and discard
the rest. Remove gill and eyes
from the head. Cut off the head
and remove the fillet from the
backbone. Place the fillet skin-
side down and score in several
places to cut unpleasant fish
bones.

* dish made of sautéed onions, tomatoes and green peppers. A Hungarian speciality.

To cook

Place the head, fins and bones
of the fish in a pot. Add thinly
sliced onion, but no fat. Salt and
add 100 ml/½ cup water. Cook
first over low heat and then over
high heat, stirring constantly until the mixture turns grey and at-
tains a pulpy consistency. Add
both types of paprika and the
letcho. Simmer for a few more
minutes and dilute with 2 1/2 qt
cold water. Cook over low heat
for 45–50 minutes, drain, and
put through a strainer. Salt fillets and roll slightly and sprinkle
with sweet paprika. Add to the
soup and simmer gently for
another 10 minutes. Serve at
once.

1–3. Filleting I.
4. Cutting up the fish to remove small bones

Golden dragon spaghetti

Ingredients

400 g/14 oz calf's brain
400 g/14 oz chicken
150 g/5 oz pickled gherkins
1 medium onion
1 tbsp ground coriander seed
salt, ground black pepper
300 g/10 oz spaghetti
150 g/5 oz grated Parmesan
cheese
70 g/3 oz butter

To prepare

Cook chicken in beef broth.
Bone and finely chop or mince.
Carefully remove membranes of
the brain and chop very fine.
Dice peeled onion and gherkins.

To cook

Sauté onion lightly in 2 tbsp
butter. Add the brain and cook
8 to 10 minutes over low heat.
Add gherkins, minced chicken
and season with salt, pepper
and coriander seed.
Cook spaghetti in salted water.
Rinse under running cold water
and drain well. Combine with
a little melted butter, salt and
place in an ovenproof dish.
Warm up in hot oven before
serving. Pile ragout on top of
the spaghetti and sprinkle with
grated Parmesan cheese.

Chinese cabbage salad

Ingredients

600 g/1¼ lb Chinese cabbage
3 cloves garlic, 1 tbsp salad oil
2 tbsp vinegar, 1 tsp sugar
salt, ground black pepper
ground caraway seed

To prepare

Separate the cabbage leaves
and wash thoroughly. Shred
and salt. Let stand for 10 minutes. Press out excess water. *To
make salad dressing* combine
finely crushed garlic, caraway
seed, black pepper, salt, wine
vinegar, water and sugar.
Sprinkle cabbage with the oil,
pour salad dressing over it and
chill before serving. This salad
will keep for 2 to 3 days.

The dragon's secret

Ingredients

2 chicken breasts
2 bananas, 2 eggs
3 tbsp flour, 4 tbsp breadcrumbs
salt, 500 ml/1 pint cooking oil
150 g/5 oz Brussels sprouts
100 g/4 oz sweet kernel of corn
100 g/4 oz peas
100 g/4 oz pimento
50 g/2 oz butter
ground black pepper

To prepare

Bone the chicken breasts and flatten carefully. Salt both sides. Place half a banana on each and roll up. Steam the vegetables and corn in butter for a few minutes. Season with salt and pepper. Cover and cook in 100 ml/ ½ cup water until tender.

To cook

Carefully bread the rolled up breasts of chicken by dipping first in flour, then in egg and finally in the breadcrumbs. Fry in hot cooking oil and serve with steamed vegetables.

1. Halving chicken breast
2. Boning with the hand
3. Rolling up the bananas
4. Breading

Rump steak in tomato purée

Ingredients

600 g/1¼ lb rump steak
150 g/5 oz carrots
100 g/4 oz parsnips
2 medium onions
oil for the marinade
400 g/14 oz Brussels sprouts
50 g/2 oz butter, 100 g/4 oz tomato purée
salt, ground black pepper
ground basil
200 ml/1 cup dry red wine
1 tbsp sugar

To prepare

Cut rump steak into four slices
of equal size. Cover with oil and
keep in refrigerator for 2 to
3 days.
Skin and finely chop the onion.
Clean and grate the carrots and
parsnips.

To cook

Sauté the onion in cooking oil
used for the marinade. Add the
grated vegetables. Season with
salt and pepper. Add a little water and cook. Sprinkle with basil
and boil together with the tomato purée and red wine until
the liquid is reduced to sauce
consistency.
Add sugar to taste.
Toss the Brussels sprouts in hot
butter. Season with salt and
pepper, cover and cook in a
little water. Salt the meat and
fry in a little oil till rare, medium
or well done.
Pour sauce over the meat and
serve with the Brussels sprouts.

Quails stuffed with mushrooms

Ingredients

8 quails, 8 quail's eggs
400 g/14 oz mushrooms
3 medium onions
1 bunch parsley, 2 egg whites
2 tbsp flour, 50 g/2 oz butter
200 ml/1 cup heavy cream, salt
ground black pepper, 1 tbsp lard

To prepare

Dry-pluck and draw the quails.
Sprinkle with salt both inside
and out. Clean the mushrooms
and wash in several changes of
water. Chop very fine or grate
⅓ of the mushrooms. Slice the
rest very thinly. Finely chop
parsley and onion. Hard-boil
and peel quail's eggs.

To cook

Sauté 1 tbsp onion in 20 g/¾ oz
butter. Add the grated mushrooms and season with salt and
pepper. Sauté until liquid evaporates. Sprinkle with 1 tbsp flour
and a little parsley. Remove
from heat and add 2 egg whites,
one after the other. Stuff quails
with mushroom mixture, place
in greased oven dish and roast
in hot oven for approx. 50 minutes. Baste frequently.
Sauté the rest of the onions in
30 g/1¼ oz butter. Add the
sliced mushrooms. Season with
salt and pepper and reduce liquid as above. Sprinkle with
1 tbsp flour and the rest of the
parsley. Add the heavy cream
and enough water to give
a sauce consistency after
thorough boiling.
Serve the quails with mushroom
sauce and potato croquettes.
(See recipe for wild duck with
quince.) Garnish with hard-
boiled quail's eggs.

**Wels
with garlic**

Ingredients

700 g/1½ lb fillet of wels
4 cloves garlic
600 g/1¼ lb fresh spinach
50 g/2 oz butter
100 ml/½ cup cooking oil
200 ml/1 cup heavy cream
150 g/5 oz carrots
150 g/5 oz parsnip
salt, ground black pepper
1 tbsp flour, 1 lemon

To prepare

Cut the boned and skinned fish fillet into 8 slices of equal size. Sprinkle with salt. Clean and wash spinach. Place it in boiling water and drain immediately. Shred the cleaned vegetables and cook in salted water for 10 minutes. Keep warm until serving time.
Crush the garlic.

To cook

Dip the fish fillets in flour and fry in hot cooking oil or lard until golden brown.
Melt the butter, add the scalded spinach and cook, stirring constantly. Season with salt, pepper and crushed garlic. Add the heavy cream, cook for another 15 minutes. Serve with a garnish of shredded vegetables. Place slices of fish on a long serving plate and sprinkle with gravy from the pan combined with half the crushed garlic. Trickle lemon juice on fish according to taste.

41

1. Piling filling on meat
2–3. Roll up tightly in aluminium foil

Dragon moufflon

Ingredients

1 kg/2½ lb leg or shoulder
of moufflon
200 g/7 oz chestnuts, fresh
50 g/2 oz smoked bacon
150 g/5 oz carrots
100 g/4 oz parsnips
2 medium onions
50 g/2 oz mushrooms
200 ml/1 cup dry red wine
salt, ground black pepper
thyme, bay leaf, 1 tsp sugar
1 lemon, 1 tbsp mustard

To prepare

Bone the meat and open with
a sharp knife. Gently pound until it is 1 cm/½ inch thick and
about twice the size of your
palm. Trim the edges to obtain
a regular oblong shape. Mince
the trimmed-off pieces and combine with finely diced bacon,
shelled and skinned chestnuts
(see p. 62.), 1 egg and diced
mushrooms. Season with salt,
pepper and thyme. Place the
mixture on the meat, roll up
tightly and wrap in aluminium
foil. Clean the vegetables and
cut lengthwise in four.

To cook

Lightly sauté the onion in a little
lard. Add the vegetables and
stew for a few minutes. Pour in
the red wine. Season with salt,
black pepper, bay leaf, thyme,
lemon juice. Put in stuffed moufflon roll, cover and cook until
tender. If the stewing broth
evaporates, add water. Tear up
foil after the first half hour of
cooking. When meat is tender
(about an hour), remove it, together with some of the vegetables. Put the rest of the broth
and vegetables through a blender, bring to boil once more, add
mustard and the diced cooked
vegetables.

To serve: place each slice of
meat on a "napkin dumpling"
cut about 2 cm/1 inch thick. Top
with vegetable sauce.

Napkin dumplings
Ingredients: 6 rolls, 3 eggs,
1 bunch parsley, 2 tbsp breadcrumbs, 200 ml/1 cup milk,
50 g/2 oz lard, salt
Dice rolls and sprinkle with hot
milk. Season with salt, pepper
and chopped parsley. Fold in
the eggs and the breadcrumbs.
Place mixture on a slightly buttered cloth napkin and shape into a cylindrical form. Tightly roll
up and cook in salted water until done (about 20 minutes).

Székely goulash

Ingredients

700 g/1½ lb shoulder of pig
700 g/1½ lb sauerkraut
100 g/4 oz smoked bacon
1 tsp sweet paprika
dash hot paprika
150 g/5 oz onion, 2 cloves garlic
200 ml/1 cup sour cream
1 tbsp flour, whole black pepper
1 bay leaf, salt

To prepare

Cut the meat into cubes and
chop fine the smoked bacon and
onion. If sauerkraut is too sour,
rinse in cold water.

To cook

Fry the fat of the bacon (the
cracklings remain in the dish)
and sauté onion in it. Remove
from heat, let stand for a few
seconds and sprinkle with the
sweet and hot paprika. Add
100 ml/½ cup water and boil for
a few minutes. Add the meat,
salt and cook, uncovered, together with the bay leaf,
crushed garlic and black pepper.
Replace evaporated water as
necessary, but never cover the
meat. Add the cabbage after the
first ½ hour of cooking and continue cooking until tender.
Stir the flour into the sour
cream until smooth, add to the
goulash and bring to the boil
once more.

Cottage cheese doughnuts with banana cream

Ingredients

500 g/1 lb cottage cheese
2 eggs, 200 g/7 oz sugar
250 g/9 oz flour
100 ml/½ cup sour cream
100 g/4 oz butter
300 ml/1½ cups cooking oil
for frying
500 g/1 lb bananas
200 ml/1 cup heavy cream
1 lemon, grated lemon rind

To prepare

Put cottage cheese through
potato masher. Whip the butter
until creamy. Add the 2 eggs,
one at a time, the sour cream,
the flour, sugar, grated lemon
rind and work together with
your fingers. Put bananas, heavy
cream and a little lemon juice
through blender and chill in refrigerator.
Roll the cottage cheese dough
on a floured board to about
2 cm/1 in thickness. Cut with
biscuit cutters and fry both sides
until golden brown.

Makó onion soup

Ingredients

6 large onions
50 ml/¼ cup cooking oil
100 ml/½ cup dry white wine
2 bay leaves
4 cloves garlic
10–15 whole black peppers
50 g/2 oz butter
2 croissants
1 bunch chives
1 bouillon cube
salt

To prepare

Peel and dice the onions. Pile black pepper, bay leaves and 3 cloves of slightly crushed garlic on a piece of linen. Tie ends tightly together. Slice the croissants into thick rings. Fry both sides in hot butter until brown and rub with garlic while still hot. Set aside until serving time.

To cook

Sauté the diced onions until golden brown in hot cooking oil. Add 100 ml/½ cup white wine and simmer for a few minutes. Add 1½ l/1½ qt water, the pouch of spices and the bouillon cube. Cook over low heat for 30 minutes, removing the froth from time to time. Salt to taste. Remove spice pouch before serving.
Serve onion soup with fried croissant slices and sprinkle with freshly cut chives.

Strudel with brain

Ingredients

600 g/1¼ lb calf's or beef's brain
600 g/1¼ lb savoy cabbage,
1 lemon
frozen prepared strudel dough
salt
50 g/2 oz butter

To prepare

Remove brain membranes, salt and sprinkle with lemon juice. Remove outer leaves from savoy cabbage, cut out the stalk and immerse in boiling salted water for 4 to 5 minutes. Remove from water, peel off each leaf individually and dry in cloth napkin.

To cook

Unfold ready to use strudel dough over a clean table-cloth and sprinkle with melted butter. Spread out boiled savoy leaves in the middle. Spread prepared brain lengthwise over cabbage leaves and roll up with the help of the cloth. Brush top with melted butter and bake in medium-hot oven for 35 to 40 minutes.

1. Spreading the leaves
2. Rolling up the strudel
3. Brushing with melted butter

Ingredients

500 g/1 lb canned green beans
1 bunch radishes
150 g/5 oz cucumbers
200 g/7 oz tomatoes
3 tbsp cooking oil
150 g/5 oz blue cheese, salt
ground black pepper
1 bunch parsley
1 lemon

To prepare

Clean and finely slice the radishes and cucumber. Grate the cheese and finely chop the parsley.

Place radishes and cucumber into a salad bowl. Salt and set aside in a cold place for ½ hour. Mix oil, lemon juice, pinch of ground black pepper, parsley, drained green beans, grated cheese and tomato wedges with the cooled radishes and cucumber.

Mixed salad with cheese

Breast of turkey, Messalina

Ingredients

1 [800 g/1¾ lb] breast of turkey
150 g/5 oz champignon mushrooms
100 g/4 oz pineapple, tinned
200 ml/1 cup heavy cream
1 medium onion
1 tbsp curry powder
1 tbsp paprika purée
or sweet paprika
50 g/2 oz butter, 1 egg
200 g/7 oz rice, 50 g/2 oz lard
1 tbsp flour

To prepare

Bone breast of turkey and cut in
half. Slit open each half with
a sharp knife and shape into
a rectangular form. Grind
trimmed-off pieces and combine
with salt, pepper, egg and paprika purée or sweet paprika.
Skin and chop the onion and
dice the mushrooms and
pineapple.
Wash, drain and dry the rice.

To cook

Slightly flatten the turkey breast,
sprinkle with salt and top with
the seasoned meat. Roll up
tightly and wrap each roll in
aluminium foil. Cook for 1 hour
in bouillon or stock. Heat rice in
1 tbsp lard, add 350 ml/¾ pt hot
water, salt and cover. Boil for
5 minutes. Remove from heat
and let stand for 15 to 20 minutes. You will obtain fluffy tender rice without having to stir it.
Sauté onion in a little butter.
Add the mushrooms and a few
minutes later the pineapple.
Sprinkle with curry powder and
flour. Add the heavy cream and
a quantity of water that will give
a sauce consistency after boiling. Finally, season with salt and
pour on the sliced stuffed breast
of turkey. Serve with the cooked
rice.

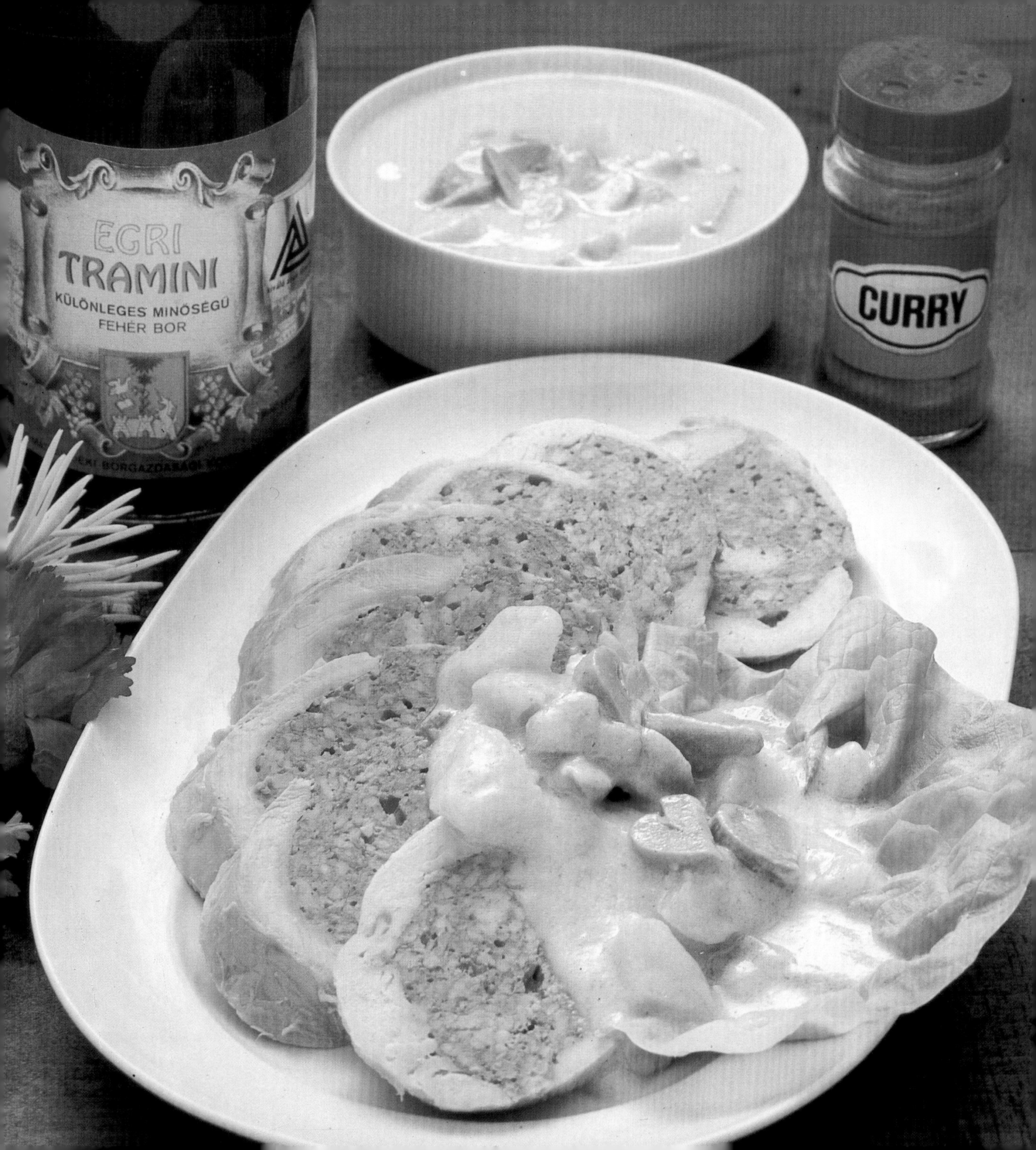
EGRI
TRAMINI
KÜLÖNLEGES MINŐSÉGŰ
FEHÉR BOR
CURRY

Fillet mignon with Dover sauce

Ingredients

600 g/1¼ lb fillet mignon
cooking oil for the marinade
4 egg yolks, 100 g/4 oz butter
100 ml/½ cup ketchup
100 ml/½ cup heavy cream
150 g/5 oz carrots, 150 g/5 oz
parsnips
300 g/10 oz potatoes
1 bunch parsley, salt
ground black pepper, basil

To prepare

Remove film from steak. Cover
with oil and marinade in refrigerator for 2 to 3 days. Clean
carrots and parsnips, cut
lengthwise and boil in salted
water. Repeat process with the
potatoes cut into wedges. Finely
chop the parsley.

To cook

Combine egg yolks with a little
salt, the ketchup and the basil in
a bowl or oven-proof dish. Add
the heavy cream, place over
boiling water and whip till it
thickens. Remove from steam
bath and stir in the melted butter by the tablespoon. Keep hot
until serving time.
Remove steak from marinade
and drain. Cut into slices 2 cm/
1 in thick. Season with salt and
pepper and fry in 1 tbsp very
hot cooking oil. Turn the meat
only once, when the underside
is browned. Serve with finely
chopped parsley, boiled
potatoes, vegetables and Dover
sauce.

1. Removing the film before marinading

Knuckle of pork with cabbage

Ingredients

2 knuckles of pork
400 g/14 oz cabbage
200 g/7 oz smoked bacon
3 medium onions
2 cloves garlic
salt, ground caraway seed
1 tbsp vinegar

To prepare

Thinly slice the cabbage and the skinned onion. Combine, sprinkle with salt and let stand for ½ hour.
Dice the bacon and crush the garlic.
Soak an earthenware casserole in water for 10 minutes. Salt the meat 1½ hours before cooking.

To cook

Squeeze out the salted cabbage. Combine with the bacon, finely crushed garlic, caraway seed and vinegar. Place in earthenware casserole and top with the knuckle of pig. Cover and bake in preheated oven for 1½ hours.
To serve: Bone the meat and cut into slices 2 cm/1 in thick.

Sturgeon in dilled mushroom sauce

Ingredients

4 [1 kg/2½ lb] sturgeon
500 ml/1 pint cooking oil for frying
600 g/1¼ lb potatoes, dill
250 g/8 oz mushrooms
200 ml/1 cup heavy cream,
2 tbsp flour
salt, ground black pepper
1 onion, 50 g/2 oz butter

To prepare

Draw the fish and cut off thorny scales along the spine. Remove the notochord. Sprinkle with salt inside and out and fasten head and tail with trussing needle. Dip in flour.
Clean mushrooms and wash in plenty of water. Slice thinly. Finely chop the dill and onion. Peel the potatoes, cut into wedges and cook in salted water. Drain well.

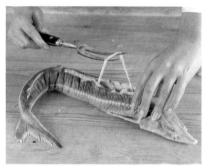

To cook

Sauté the onion in butter until golden brown, add the mushrooms and cook until broth evaporates. Sprinkle with dill, season with salt and pepper, add 1 tbsp flour, heavy cream and a little water. Boil until liquid is reduced to sauce consistency. Fry the fish in hot cooking oil. Place mushroom sauce on serving plates, top with the fried fish and garnish with boiled potatoes.

1. Cutting lengthwise
2. Removing the notochord
3. Fastening with needle or other implement

Pheasant stuffed with chestnuts

Ingredients

1 pheasant, 500 g/1 lb chestnuts
300 g/10 oz smoked bacon
4 apples
400 g/14 oz Brussels sprouts
50 g/2 oz butter
1 roll, salt, marjoram
ground nutmeg, 1 egg
1 tbsp lard

To prepare

Dry-pluck and eviscerate the
pheasant. Sprinkle with salt
both inside and out. Sprinkle the
cavity with marjoram. Score the
tops of the chestnuts, place in
a hot oven and bake until they
open up fully. Peel and chop
finely.
Cut the smoked bacon into large
thin slices.

To cook

Soak roll in water, squeeze it
out and combine with the chestnuts, egg, a little salt and
ground nutmeg. Place this mixture in the pheasant's abdominal cavity. Truss the legs with
a skewer. Cover the pheasant
with slices of smoked bacon and
wrap up tightly with aluminium
foil. Place in a greased oven-
dish and bake in a moderately
hot oven for 1½ hours. Remove
core from the apples and put
them in with the pheasant for
the last 15 to 20 minutes of baking. When done, slice the
apples. Toss the Brussels
sprouts in melted butter. Season
with salt and pepper. Add a little
water, cover and cook until
tender.
To serve: remove foil, carve the
pheasant and garnish with
baked apple and cooked Brussels sprouts.

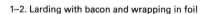
1–2. Larding with bacon and wrapping in foil

Székely mixed pickles

Ingredients

500 g/1 lb sauerkraut
100 g/3½ oz carrots
150 g/5 oz gherkins
100 g/3½ oz marinated pepper
3 cherry peppers
150 g/5 oz onion, 1 bunch dill
1 tbsp sugar, 2 tbsp salad oil
3 tbsp vinegar, salt

To prepare

Wash cabbage and press out excess liquid. Slice very fine or shred peeled carrots and gherkins. Peel onion, cut it lengthwise and slice very thin. Salt and set aside for 10 to 15 minutes. Shred marinated pepper and chop dill. Use whole cherry-peppers.
Dissolve a little sugar in ½ l/1 pint cold water and combine with vinegar, cooking oil and chopped dill. Mix prepared ingredients in a bowl and pour salad dressing on top. Make a larger quantity if you like and store in refrigerator.

Orange delight

Ingredients

4 oranges, 3 egg whites
200 g/7 oz granulated sugar
200 ml/1 cup milk, 1 tbsp flour
100 ml/½ cup heavy cream
100 ml/½ cup orange liqueur
grated orange rind

To prepare

Peel and section 2 oranges. Squeeze out the juice of the other two.
Blend the lukewarm milk, 1 tbsp flour, and 100 g sugar until smooth. Boil with the orange juice and heavy cream. Stir in the liqueur just before serving. Whip the egg whites with 50 g/2 oz sugar until stiff. Shape into rings with a spoon and cook each side for 2 minutes in ½ l/1 pt simmering water sweetened with 2 tbsp sugar.

To serve

Ladle warm orange sauce into small bowls and decorate with orange sections. Using a slotted spoon remove the stiff egg whites from the surface of the cooking water and place on top of the orange sauce. Sprinkle with grated orange rind.

1. Cutting off the ends
2. Peeling
3–4. Section and remove membranes

Ingredients

400 g/1 lb potatoes
2 medium onions
100 g/3½ oz parsnip
50 g/2 oz celeriac
2 cloves garlic
1 bunch parsley, salt
ground black pepper
1 tbsp lard

To prepare

Peel and dice potatoes. Clean and chop vegetables and onion. Finely chop parsley and garlic.

To cook

Sauté vegetables and onion in 1 tbsp lard for 8 to 10 minutes. Season with salt and pepper. Add 1 l/1 qt cold water and cook over low heat for 20 minutes. Add potatoes, garlic and parsley. Serve as soon as potatoes are cooked.

68

Cold goose liver

Ingredients

500 g/1 lb goose liver
500 g/1 lb goose fat
3 onions
500 ml/1 pint milk, salt
whole black pepper
2 cloves garlic

To prepare

Soak liver in salted milk for
1 day. Dice the goose fat, fry it
and remove cracklings. Skin the
onion and cut into wedges.

To cook

Place the onion, the peppercorns, a dash of salt, garlic and,
finally, the goose liver in the hot
goose fat. Cover and fry over
low heat for 40 to 45 minutes.
Carefully remove the liver and
place in deep glass bowl. Strain
the fat, cool to room tempera-
ture and pour over liver. Chill in
refrigerator.
Serve the thinly sliced goose
liver with toast, decorated with
salad or fruit compote.

Beet salad with mayonnaise

Ingredients

1 beet, 200 g/7 oz apples
50 g/2 oz horseradish
2 egg yolks
½ lemon
100 ml/½ cup dry white wine
1 tsp mustard
300 ml/1½ cups salad oil
1 tsp castor sugar
salt, 100 ml/½ cup sour cream
1 tbsp vinegar

To prepare

Wash beetroot and cook in salted water. Slice thin and sprinkle with a little vinegar. Peel and grate the apples.
To make the mayonnaise add mustard, salt and lemon juice to the egg yolks. Add oil very slowly, stirring constantly. Sweeten with castor sugar to taste, thin slightly with white wine and, finally, mix in the sour cream.
Combine sauce with grated apple and grated horseradish. Carefully mix with sliced beet. Chill in refrigerator for a few hours. Serve with fish, roast lamb or poultry dishes.

Leg of goose with apple cabbage

Ingredients

1 kg/2¼ lb leg of goose
600 g/1¼ lb red cabbage
200 g/7 oz apples
5 onions, 400 g/14 oz potatoes
2 tbsp vinegar
1 tbsp sugar, 3 cloves garlic, salt
marjoram, ground caraway seed
1 tbsp lard, 100 ml/½ cup dry
red wine

To prepare

Rub legs of goose with salt, marjoram and salted garlic. Place in greased oven dish and bake for about 1 hour in a moderate oven.
Core, thinly slice and salt the cabbage.
Cut half the skinned onion into wedges, the other half into thin slices.
Peel the potatoes and cut into wedges. Thinly slice the skinned apples.

To cook

Caramellize sugar in 1 tbsp lard. (Stir constantly in hot lard until the sugar melts and becomes light brown.) Add the sliced onions and sauté for a few minutes. Finally, add the sliced cabbage and the apple. When the cabbage is half done, add the red wine and vinegar. Continue cooking until cabbage is done. When the leg of goose is half done, add the onion and the potatoes and roast until the meat is crispy brown.
Serve leg of goose either whole or cut up, together with the potatoes and the apple cabbage.

Stuffed loin of pork

Ingredients

800 g/1¾ lb loin of pork
50 g/2 oz diced green pepper
50 g/2 oz green peas
50 g/2 oz sweet corn, tinned
1 egg, 80 g/3 oz lean ham
1 bunch parsley, 500 g/1 lb
potatoes
100 g/4 oz butter, 50 g/2 oz
lard
200 ml/1 cup milk
50 g/2 oz semolina, salt
ground black pepper

To prepare

Scald and drain green peppers
and green peas.
Dice the lean ham and finely
chop the parsley. Peel the
potatoes, cut in half and boil in
salted water. Drain well.
With the tip of a sharp knife
pierce the center of the meat
lengthwise and salt.

To cook

Whip 50 g/2 oz soft butter until
creamy. Add 1 egg and beat until smooth. Add the semolina,
corn, green peas, ham, diced
green pepper and parsley. Season with salt and pepper and
stuff the meat. Secure each end
with trussing needle or skewer.
Roast in lightly greased oven
pan in a moderate oven. Baste
frequently. Set aside for 4 to
5 minutes after roasting.
Serve with mashed potatoes.
Mash the boiled potatoes, add
50 g/2 oz butter, salt and
200 ml/1 cup milk, whip with
a fork or heavy whisk until
creamy.

1. Piercing the meat
2. Stuffing the meat
3. Fastening with skewer (trussing needle)

Ingredients

2 wild ducks, 5 quinces
3 medium onions, salt
marjoram, 50 g/2 oz butter
400 g/14 oz potatoes, 3 eggs
5 tbsp flour, 4 tbsp breadcrumbs
400 ml/2 cups cooking oil
200 ml/1 cup dry white wine
2 tbsp lard

Wild duck with quince

To prepare
Pluck and draw the wild ducks. Sprinkle with salt inside and out and sprinkle marjoram inside abdominal cavity. Pare and slice 4 quinces. Place them in abdominal cavity.
Peel and slice onions.
Cook unpeeled potatoes. Peel and mash.

To cook
Place wild ducks and sliced onion into greased oven dish. Roast in a moderately hot oven for about 1 hour. Baste frequently.
Combine mashed potatoes with 2 tbsp flour, 2 eggs, salt, ground nutmeg and shape into balls the size of a nut. Dip into flour, egg and breadcrumbs and fry in hot cooking oil.
Melt the butter, add the rest of the sliced quince and wine, cover and cook.
Remove quince stuffing from the wild ducks. Carve the meat and serve with potato croquettes and stewed quinces.

1. Scoring
2. Shaping the fish
3. Serving the fish

Fried pike-perch

Ingredients

2 [1½ kg/3 lb] pike-perch
500 ml/1 pint oil for frying
salt, 600 g/1¼ lb potatoes
50 g/2 oz butter
1 bunch parsley
200 ml/1 cup mayonnaise
(see recipe for beets with
mayonnaise)
100 ml/½ cup sour cream
100 ml/½ cup dry white wine
2 lemons, powdered sugar
2 tbsp flour

To prepare

Peel, dice and cook potatoes in salted water. Drain well. Remove scales from fish, draw and remove gill. Make incisions at 1 cm/½ in intervals on both sides along the spine. Sprinkle with salt inside and out. Blend mayonnaise with sour cream and white wine until smooth. Season with salt, powdered sugar and lemon juice according to taste. Chill before serving.

To cook

Shape fish into a crescent shape by turning up the two ends. Fasten with skewer (trussing needle) pierced through the neck and tail of the fish. Sprinkle both sides with flour and fry until golden brown. Sauté the chopped parsley in butter and mix in the potatoes. Place fish with head and tail turned up on a serving plate and garnish with the potatoes. Serve with sauce tartare.

**Freshwater crab
with dill sauce**

Ingredients

12 crabs, 400 g/14 oz cucumber
1 bunch dill, 1 bunch parsley
200 ml/1 cup heavy cream
100 ml/½ cup dry white wine
4 quail's eggs, 1½ tbsp butter
100 g/4 oz flour, 3 cloves garlic
caraway seed, salt
1 lemon
100 ml/½ cup cooking oil

To prepare

Boil the quail's eggs for about
10 minutes. Immerse in cold water and peel.
Wash cucumbers, slice into
2 cm/1 in thick rings and
sprinkle with salt.
Finely chop the dill and parsley
and reserve parsley stems.

To cook

Prepare a roux from 2 tbsp flour
and the butter. Add the dill, the
fresh cream and the white wine.
Season with salt and lemon
juice and boil until liquid is reduced to sauce consistency. Dip
sliced cucumber in flour and fry
both sides in a little cooking oil.
Twist the middle section of the
tail of each live crab and pull,
together with entrails. Place
crabs, one by one, into 1½ l/
1½ qt boiling salted water seasoned with caraway seed, garlic
and parsley stems. Boil for
8 minutes and serve, whole, at
once. Use a nutcracker for open-
ing the claws and cracking the
shells. Serve with fried
cucumbers, hard-boiled quail's
eggs and dill sauce.

Pancakes with vanilla fruit cream

Ingredients

600 g/1¼ lb fruit compote
(pineapple, sour cherries,
grapes)
100 ml/½ cup Triple Sec
50 g/2 oz castor sugar
Pancakes:
200 ml/1 cup milk
200 ml/1 cup soda water
2 eggs, 200 g/7 oz flour
cooking oil for frying
Vanilla sauce:
1 egg yolk, 50 g/2 oz sugar
2 tsp vanilla sugar
100 ml/½ cup milk

To prepare

Sprinkle the drained fruit with
the liqueur. Beat 1 egg yolk
50 g/2 oz sugar and vanilla
sugar until well blended. Add
hot milk and boil to creamy consistency over steam.
Prepare pancake batter from the
milk, the 2 eggs and the flour
and bake. (You will get about
10 pancakes.)
Carefully mix fruit and vanilla
cream and fill pancakes. Roll
them up and sprinkle with powdered sugar. Serve hot.

Ingredients

300 g/10 oz mushrooms
2 tbsp sweet paprika
1 onion
ground black pepper, salt
200 ml/1 cup sour cream
50 g/2 oz flour
1 tbsp lard, 1 egg

To prepare

Cut off earthy part of the mushroom stems. Wash thoroughly in several changes of water. Remove mushrooms from surface of water. Slice very thin, including the stems.
Dice the peeled onion.
Salt egg slightly and prepare a paste mixing the egg with 1 tbsp flour.

To cook

Sauté onion in 1 tbsp lard. Add sliced mushrooms, salt and simmer until juices released by the mushrooms evaporate. Sprinkle with paprika and ground black pepper. Add 1½ l/1½ qt water and cook for 15 to 20 minutes. Stir 2 level tbsp flour into sour cream. Add to soup and cook for another 5 minutes. Finally, slowly trickle the prepared egg paste mixture into the soup through a thin-stemmed funnel or a pierced plastic bag.

Mushrooms topped with quail's eggs

Ingredients

12 quail's eggs
12 mushroom caps
1 tbsp butter, salt
ground black pepper
1 bunch parsley
200 ml/1 cup ketchup

To prepare

Skin and wash mushrooms.
Carefully break off or cut out
stems. (Use these for another
dish.) Season both sides of
mushroom caps with salt and
pepper.
Finely chop parsley.

To cook

Heat 1 tbsp lard in a pan. Fry
mushrooms' rounded side up
for 5 to 6 minutes. Turn and
sprinkle with chopped parsley.
Top each mushroom with
a quail's egg. Fry until eggs are
done.
Put some lukewarm ketchup on
each plate and place the mushrooms on top.
This dish is an excellent hors
d'œuvre, but with buttered toast
it makes a light evening meal.

Black radish salad

Ingredients

200 g/7 oz black radishes
200 g/7 oz lean ham, sliced
100 g/3½ oz leeks, 2 eggs
2 tbsp salad oil
4 tbsp apple vinegar
1 bunch parsley, salt
ground black pepper

To prepare

Clean and thinly slice radishes.
Cut slices into strips. Slice white
part of the leeks into thin rings.
Add the radishes, season with
salt and pepper, and set aside
for 10 minutes. Press out excess
liquid and combine with vinegar, oil, finely chopped parsley,
shredded ham and sliced, hard-
boiled eggs. Mix carefully and
chill before serving.

Chicken with horseradish

Ingredients

1 small chicken
1 medium onion
100 g/4 oz carrots and parsnip
300 g/10 oz rice
1 tbsp lard, 100 g/4 oz green peas
100 g/4 oz horseradish
½ lemon, 50 g/2 oz butter
2 tbsp flour, salt
whole black pepper
100 ml/½ cup dry white wine
1 bunch parsley

To prepare

Clean and grate the horseradish and sprinkle with lemon to preserve white color. Cook the chicken together with the onion, vegetables, salt and black pepper in enough water to cover ingredients.
Chop the parsley.

To cook

Remove the chicken and drain. Strain the broth.
Make a light roux from the flour and butter. Add two-thirds of the grated horseradish. Add the wine and the chicken broth. Reduce to sauce consistency. Salt to taste, add the carved cooked chicken and serve piping hot. Top with grated horseradish and serve with cooked rice mixed with green peas.
Heat the rice in a little lard, salt and add ½ l/1 pint boiling water. Add the green peas, cover, and boil for 5 minutes. Remove from heat and let stand for 15 to 20 minutes. Stir in the finely chopped parsley.

Ingredients

8 slices pork chops, with bone
50 g/2 oz lard
100 g/4 oz blue cheese
2 rolls, 1 bunch parsley
1 tbsp breadcrumbs
600 g/1¼ lb savoy cabbage
salt, ground black pepper
ground caraway seed
1 tbsp flour, 1 tbsp butter

To prepare

Grate the cheese and finely
chop the parsley.
Soak rolls in cold water and
squeeze out. Cut out the stalk
and quarter the savoy cabbage
and cook in boiling salted water
for 5 minutes. Drain well.

To cook

Salt the pork chops, dip in flour
and fry both sides in hot lard.
Top with mixture of cheese and
soaked roll, parsley, breadcrumbs and pepper. Grill for 10
to 15 minutes.
Braise the boiled cabbage in
a little butter, salt and ground
caraway seed for 5 minutes.
Serve together with the cheese-
topped pork chops.

Pork chops with blue cheese

Haunch of venison, Esterházy style

Ingredients

1 kg/2½ lb haunch of venison
200 g/7 oz smoked bacon
3 medium onions
300 g/10 oz carrots
300 g/10 oz parsnips
200 ml/1 cup sour cream
1 tbsp mustard, 1 tsp sugar
1 tbsp flour, 1 bay leaf
salt, whole black pepper
1 lemon
200 ml/1 cup dry white wine
500 ml/1 pint cooking oil

To prepare

Remove film from meat 3 to
4 days before cooking. Lard
generously with strips of
smoked bacon and marinate in
oil in a cool place. Cut half the
cleaned carrots and parsnips into long strips and cook in boiling salted water for 10 minutes.
Set aside until serving time.
Chop skinned onion and the rest
of the vegetables.

To cook

Pre-fry marinated haunch of
venison in a little hot cooking
oil, on all sides. Set aside for
a while. Sauté onion and vegetables in the same oil. Add salt,
bay leaf, peppercorns, dilute
with wine and ½ l/1 pt of water.
Bring to the boil, add the meat,
cover and cook until tender. Remove the meat and carve it. Remove vegetables and put them
through a sieve. Replace them
in the strained stewing liquid
and bring to the boil once more.
Add well-blended mixture of
flour and sour cream. Season
with a little lemon juice, mustard and sugar. Serve the carved
meat in this sauce and top with
cooked vegetable strips and roll
dumplings.

Roll dumplings

Ingredients: 6 rolls, 2 eggs,
200 ml/1 cup milk, 1 bunch
parsley, salt, ground black pepper, 2 tbsp breadcrumbs
To prepare: dice rolls and scald
with milk. Season with salt, pepper and chopped parsley. Add
the eggs and breadcrumbs and
knead. Shape dumplings with
wet hands and cook in salted
boiling water for 10 to 20 minutes. Keep warm in this cooking
water until serving time.

Carp à la Dorozsma

Ingredients

4 [600 g/1¼ lb] fillets of carp
100 g/4 oz smoked bacon
50 g/2 oz lard, 1 medium onion
1 tbsp sweet paprika
300 ml/1½ cups sour cream,
2 tbsp flour
300 g/10 oz noodles, salt

To prepare

Fillet the fish (see recipe for fish soup).
Lard the fillets with thin strips of smoked bacon. Clean, wash and dice the mushrooms and finely chop the onion. Cook noodles in rapidly boiling salted water. Drain, rinse and mix with a little melted lard. Set aside until serving time.

To cook

Sauté the onion in a little lard until transparent. Add the mushrooms and cook until excess broth evaporates. Sprinkle with paprika, 1 tbsp flour and add 200 ml/1 cup water and 200 ml/1 cup sour cream. Salt and boil until liquid is reduced to sauce consistency.
Dip fillets of carp in flour and fry in a little hot lard.
Spread the boiled noodles in a lightly greased oven pan or oven-proof dish, cover with the fried fillets of carp, pour the mushroom sauce over them and top with sour cream. Cook in a hot oven for 15 minutes and serve at once.

1. Larding the fish
2. Layering
3. Topping with sour cream

Trout with spicy mousseline sauce

Ingredients

4 [900 g/2 lb] trout
600 g/1¼ lb potatoes
50 g/2 oz butter
100 ml/½ cup mayonnaise
(see recipe for beets with mayonnaise)
100 ml/½ cup heavy cream, salt
1 bunch parsley, 1 bunch dill
1 bunch chives, 1 lemon
200 ml/1 cup cooking oil
1 tbsp flour

To prepare

Remove scales, entrails and gill
of fish. Sprinkle with salt inside
and out and dip in flour.
Peel, dice and cook potatoes in
salted water. Drain well.
Finely chop the parsley, dill and
chives.

To cook

Sauté parsley in melted butter.
Carefully mix in the boiled
potatoes and keep hot until
serving time.
For the *mousseline sauce,* whip
heavy cream and combine with
the mayonnaise. Add the chopped dill, chives and parsley and
set aside in a cool place until
serving time.
Heat oil in skillet and fry the
trout, two at a time. Turn only
when one side is nicely brown.
Sprinkle with lemon juice and
serve with the potatoes and
spicy mousseline sauce.

Fruit salad with lemon whip

Ingredients

2 oranges, 2 bananas
1 apple, 1 pear
100 ml / ½ cup heavy cream
1 lemon
100 ml / ½ cup Triple Sec
orange liqueur
2 tbsp castor sugar

To prepare

Peel and section the oranges.
Thinly slice the skinned
bananas, apple and pear. Dissolve 1 tbsp castor sugar in the
heavy cream, add the juice of
½ lemon and whip until stiff.
Carefully combine the fruit with
the rest of the lemon juice.
Sprinkle with the liqueur and
the rest of the powdered sugar
and stir once again.
Serve in small bowls topped
with the lemon whip.

Printed in Hungary 1987
Kner Printing House, Békéscsaba